OXFORD BOOKWORMS LIBRARY
True Stories

Amelia Earhart

JANET HARDY-GOULD

Stage 2 (700 headwords)

Illustrated by Simon Gurr

Series Editor: Rachel Bladon
Founder Editors: Jennifer Bassett
and Tricia Hedge

OXFORD
UNIVERSITY PRESS

Great Clarendon Street, Oxford, OX2 6DP, United Kingdom

Oxford University Press is a department of the University of Oxford.
It furthers the University's objective of excellence in research, scholarship,
and education by publishing worldwide. Oxford is a registered trade
mark of Oxford University Press in the UK and in certain other countries

ISBN: 978 0 19 423795 6

A complete recording of this Bookworms edition of
Amelia Earhart is available on audio CD. ISBN: 978 0 19 423793 2

Printed in China

Word count (main text): 8,703 words

For more information on the Oxford Bookworms Library,
visit www.oup.com/elt/gradedreaders

ACKNOWLEDGEMENTS

*The publisher would like to thank the following for their permission to reproduce
photographs*: Corbis pp.21 (Bettman), 36 (Bettman), 50 (Reuters), 55 (Wright
Brothers' first flight/Bettman, Spirit of St. Louis over Paris/Bettman, Winnie
Mae flying near Cleveland/Bettman, seaplane flying by Statue of Liberty/The
Mariners' Museum); Getty Images pp.55 (balloon ascending over Lyon/APIC,
the first flight over the English Channel/Bob Thomas/Popperfoto, Calbraith
Perry Rodgers/APIC, the first non-stop transatlantic flight, 1919/Ann Ronan
Picture Library/Heritage Images).

Illustrations by: Simon Gurr

CONTENTS

PLACES IN THIS STORY   iv

FOREWORD   1

1   Early Adventures   2

2   First Flight   7

3   Flying High   12

4   An Important Meeting   19

5   Across the Atlantic   26

6   The Ninety-Nines   32

7   Flying Solo   37

8   Around the World   41

9   One Last Adventure   46

GLOSSARY   52

THE HISTORY OF FLIGHT   55

ACTIVITIES: Before Reading   57

ACTIVITIES: While Reading   58

ACTIVITIES: After Reading   62

ABOUT THE BOOKWORMS LIBRARY   67

PLACES IN THIS STORY

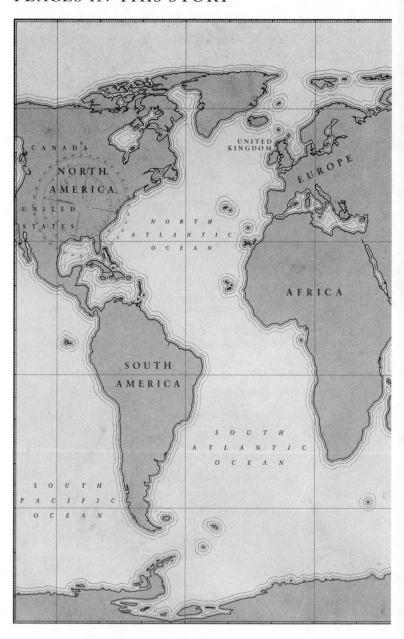

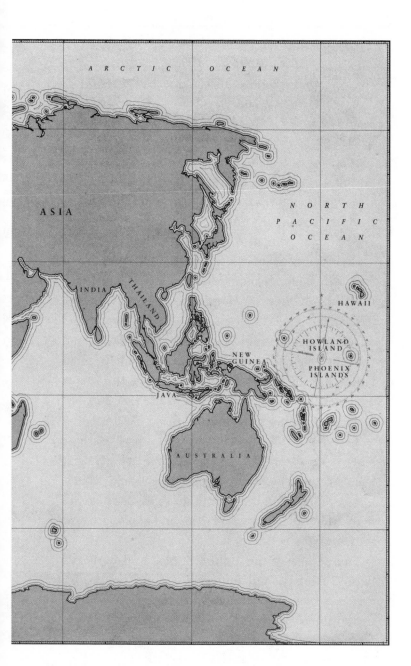

Earhart lost over Pacific

The plane of U.S. pilot Amelia Earhart has disappeared near Howland Island in the Pacific Ocean. Earhart was trying to fly around the world – the first time for any woman – and she and navigator Fred Noonan were near the end of their adventure.

Earhart and Noonan left New Guinea two days ago for the difficult and dangerous nineteen-hour flight to Howland. They were hoping to arrive at Howland in their Lockheed Electra plane in the early hours of yesterday morning. The island is very small, and U.S. ship the *Itasca* was waiting there to help them land. During the night, the people on the *Itasca* were getting radio messages from the Electra – but Earhart could not hear their replies.

The *Itasca* has not had a message from Earhart since 8:45 yesterday morning. In that last message, she said that she was looking for Howland Island, but could not find it. Since then, there has been no news from the Electra, and ships and planes are now searching the ocean for it.

The people of the United States, and Earhart's family, friends, and followers around the world, are now waiting and hoping for news of this extraordinary woman.

Chapter 1
Early Adventures

Muriel Earhart looked up at her older sister. Amelia was sitting on the top of the shed next to their large family home in Kansas City. It was a bright, windy day in 1904, and the Earhart girls were with their Uncle Carl.

Seven-year-old Amelia was cutting a piece of wood.

"Is the ride ready?" asked Muriel.

"Nearly!" cried Amelia. She looked at the long pieces of wood. They went down from the top of the shed to an old table on the ground.

"Uncle Carl!" shouted Amelia. "You know we went to St. Louis with Papa? This is just like the wonderful ride there!"

"I know," smiled Uncle Carl. "And our ride will be very exciting, too!"

At last, the ride was ready. Uncle Carl stood next to the shed with the girls. He had a large box made of wood in his hand.

"Now, who will go first on *our* ride?" he asked.

"Me, please!" answered Amelia.

"Here," said Uncle Carl. "Take the box. You go, too, Muriel, and give her a push."

The girls climbed up on the top of the shed. Amelia put the box onto the long pieces of wood and got inside it. Then Muriel gave her sister a push.

The box went slowly at first, then faster. Soon it was traveling quickly down, and when it hit the table at the end, it jumped up into the air. Amelia flew across the garden, screaming, and fell to the ground.

Uncle Carl ran across to her, but she quickly jumped up. There was a little blood on her face, and a big hole in her dress.

"Oh, Muriel," Amelia cried to her sister. "It's just like flying! I want to try it again!"

Amelia flew across the garden.

That evening, in the comfortable front room of their home, Amelia showed her mother the hole in her dress.

"Not again, Amelia," said Amy Earhart.

"Sorry, Mom," said Amelia.

"Well, we'll have to think of better clothes for you," Amy said brightly.

Some weeks later, when their father, Edwin Earhart, came home from his job at the railroad office, Amelia and Muriel ran toward him, excited. Amy stood behind them. "Papa!" cried Amelia. "Do you like our new playsuits? Mom made them."

"They're wonderful!" smiled Edwin.

"But I don't know what people will say," laughed Amy. "Girls in playsuits and not dresses!"

"It doesn't matter," said Edwin. "They're the best clothes for our daughters' adventures."

Edwin loved his girls dearly. He often took them fishing and played with them. One day, he came home with large presents.

"What have you bought now, Edwin?" asked Amy, with a worried look on her face. Her husband often spent too much on things, and there were sometimes money problems at home.

The girls opened their presents. "Oh, sleds!" they cried. "Thank you!"

"And they're not just *any* sleds," said Amelia. "We can lie on our stomachs and go *really* fast!"

"Girls in playsuits and not dresses!" laughed Amy.

Amelia and Muriel loved using their new presents on the little roads around their house. One wintry day, Amelia was going fast down a hill when Muriel suddenly shouted, "Be careful, Amelia! Somebody's coming!"

Amelia looked up. A horse pulling a cart was moving out from a side road. She cried out to the driver, but he could not hear her.

"I can't stop now," thought Amelia. So she put her head down and went through the horse's legs and out the other side.

"Amelia, you nearly died!" shouted Muriel.

"But I didn't!" laughed Amelia.

Not long after this, things began to change for the Earhart family. In 1907, Edwin Earhart took a new job in a different town – Des Moines, in Iowa. The pay was better, but the Earharts had to move home.

At first, the girls stayed with their grandmother and grandfather in Kansas. Then, after about a year, twelve-year-old Amelia and her sister moved to their mother and father's new house in Des Moines. It was smaller than their house in Kansas City, but the family was pleased to be together again.

The early years in Des Moines were happy. But after some time, Edwin had problems at the office. He was a bad worker – he was often late, and he sometimes fell asleep at his job. In the end, in 1914, Edwin came home early one day. He looked tired and sick.

"What's the matter?" asked Amy at once.

"I've lost my job," said Edwin.

And from that day, Edwin often changed jobs. The girls moved from place to place, and Amelia went to six high schools in four years.

When people later said to her, "I'm from your hometown!" she always needed to ask, "Which one?"

Chapter 2
First Flight

In 1916, Amelia started as a student at a college near Philadelphia, and her sister Muriel went to college in Toronto, Canada.

On a visit to her sister in December 1917, Amelia saw soldiers from the terrible war in Europe who were badly hurt.

"I must do something to help," she told Muriel at once. So she left college, moved to Toronto, and became a nurse in a special hospital for soldiers. She worked very long hours there, but on weekends, she went horseback riding or spent time with her new friends.

One day, she went to an air show in a field near Toronto. During the show, Amelia stood to one side with a friend, away from the crowd.

One of the pilots was flying low over the field when he saw the two young women. He began to fly at them.

"What's he doing?" cried her friend. "He's coming toward us. Run, Amelia! Run!"

But Amelia did not move. The plane came nearer and nearer and still she stood watching it. Then, at the last second, when she could see the pilot's face, it flew up and over her.

"You're extraordinary, Amelia," cried her friend, running back toward her. "Weren't you afraid?"

*The plane came nearer and nearer and
still Amelia stood watching it.*

"It was strange," said Amelia. "I was afraid, but I was
excited, too. Really excited."

In the fall of 1918, the war in Europe ended, and in the
summer of 1919, Amelia decided to go to college in New
York and become a doctor. But after six months, she
left. She wanted to do something different – something
important – but she did not know what.

Amelia's mother and father were now living in California because her father had a new business there. So in 1920, twenty-three-year-old Amelia moved to their house in California, not far from the ocean. She soon made new friends, and often went out with them to the theater or to play tennis.

One evening, Amelia came back with news of an air show.

"Let's go!" said Amelia to her father. "I went to one in Toronto. It was wonderful!"

At the show, Amelia and Edwin stood at the front of the crowd. They watched the first plane drop down suddenly from the sky and fly near the ground. It turned over and over before it climbed high in the air again.

"It's even better than the air show in Toronto!" Amelia said excitedly. She looked across at her father. "How much does it cost to learn to fly?" she asked.

"Well, I don't know," he answered. "Why are you asking?"

"I'm just interested," she said brightly.

"I'll see if I can find out," he answered, and quickly walked away. After a few minutes, he came back.

"It costs about $1,000 to learn to fly," he said. "But I've asked about plane rides. You can go on one tomorrow, if you want."

The next day, Edwin took Amelia to Rogers Field. It was one of the new airfields that were opening around

Los Angeles, and people went there to fly their planes. A tall man in a helmet, goggles, and a flying coat walked across the open field to meet them.

"Hi! I'm Frank Hawks," he said to Edwin. "And your daughter Amelia is here for a plane ride – is that right?"

"Yes," said Edwin. He gave Hawks ten dollars.

"If you like, we can take one of my men along in the plane to sit with Amelia," Hawks said. "I don't want her to jump out of the plane in the air if she's afraid!"

But before Edwin could answer, Amelia said, "You don't need to worry about that. I'll be just fine, thank you."

Hawks laughed. "OK then, if you're sure," he said, and they walked toward the plane. Then he gave Amelia some goggles, and helped her up into the cockpit.

"You sit here at the front, and I'll be behind you. The pilot always sits at the back of the plane."

Hawks got in and started the engine, and the plane began to move across the airfield. It went slowly at first, but soon it was traveling faster and faster. It shook loudly when it went over the large holes in the ground.

At last they took off, and the little plane began to climb high into the sky. With the wind in her face, Amelia looked down at the little houses, roads, and fields next to the silver ocean far below. Something happened deep inside her, and she knew at once that she wanted to learn to fly.

The flight soon came to an end, and when the plane landed on the airfield and the engine stopped, Amelia jumped down and pushed up her dirty goggles. There were two big, white circles around her eyes.

"How was that?" asked Hawks with a smile.

Amelia knew at once that she wanted to learn to fly.

Chapter 3
Flying High

"I think that I'd like to fly," Amelia told her family that evening.

"Not a bad idea," said her father, from behind the newspaper.

But when she came home a few days later and said, "I've found a flying teacher," he jumped up from his chair.

"What?" he cried. "You can't take flying lessons! Flying is dangerous – and much too expensive. And the teacher will be a man – you can't just go and learn to fly with some strange man."

Edwin's reply was not surprising. Flying was dangerous at that time, and bad accidents sometimes happened on the ground and in the air. But he could not easily stop Amelia.

A few days later, she spoke to her father again. "I've found a woman flying teacher called Neta Snook," she told him. "She's a wonderful pilot, everybody says."

"But how much are the lessons?" asked Edwin.

"$500 for twelve hours," said Amelia.

Edwin looked away. "I'm sorry, Amelia. You know what I said before. I just don't have the money."

But Amelia knew what she wanted, and in the end, Edwin could not stop her. At last, he said that she could take flying lessons if she helped at his office on Saturday mornings.

The next week, Edwin and Amelia went to an airfield called Kinner Field. They found a young woman there with short, red hair. She was wearing pants, boots, and a dirty flying coat, and she was looking into the engine of a large plane.

"Are you Neta Snook?" asked Amelia.

"Yes, that's me," she replied. "I'm the only woman around here!"

"I'm Amelia Earhart, and this is my father. I want to learn to fly," said Amelia. "Will you teach me?"

"Sure," smiled Neta. She liked this tall, fair-haired young woman at once. "Come tomorrow afternoon at two o'clock."

The next day, Amelia put on her old, brown horseback-riding pants and boots, and went to Kinner Field. Neta gave her a helmet and goggles.

"You sit in the cockpit at the front of the plane," shouted Neta, above the noise of the engine, "and I'll sit in the back. For the first lesson, we're going to stay on the ground, and I'll explain the flight controls."

Soon, Neta was showing Amelia everything inside the plane.

"What does this part do?" Amelia asked. "And how does that stick work?" She had so many questions, and she wanted to ask them all at once.

For the first few weeks, Amelia was not ready to fly the plane in the air herself, but one afternoon, when

"What does this part do?" Amelia asked.

they took off, Neta cried, "You can begin to move the controls yourself now!"

Amelia immediately began to pull the control stick in front of her, and felt the plane climb higher.

"Yes, that's it!" shouted Neta, and she told Amelia to do different things. At the end of the lesson, Neta took back the controls and landed the plane.

"Thank you!" cried Amelia. "That was so exciting!"

"You're welcome," laughed Neta. "I think you're going to be good at this."

Soon, Amelia was spending all her free time at Kinner Field, and she and Neta quickly became good friends. On sunny days, she learned how to repair the planes. When it rained, she read one of the books about flying that she always carried with her. Or sometimes she sat in one of the old sheds, and talked about planes with Neta and the other pilots.

One afternoon, Neta looked at Amelia strangely. "Your hair looks shorter," she said.

Amelia laughed. "My mom doesn't like women with short hair, so I'm cutting it a little every day. That way she doesn't see it!"

Amelia was finding more work to pay for her lessons with Neta, but she needed money for something new now.

"The thing is," she told her mother one evening, "I'd really like to buy a plane. Then people will begin to see me as a real pilot. Mr. Kinner from the airfield is selling a plane. Will you help me buy it, with the money from your family?"

"I don't know, Amelia," said her mother. "I need to think about it." But Amy did not need to think about it for very long. She gave Amelia some money, and just before her twenty-fourth birthday, in July 1921, Amelia bought the plane.

Amelia's plane was small and fast – not like Neta's big, heavy one. She loved flying in it, and called it the *Canary* because it was bright yellow, like the songbird.

Amelia had a new teacher now – an exciting pilot called John Montijo. He began to teach her about aerobatics, and with his help she made her first solo flight. Montijo was watching from the airfield with Neta when Amelia took off, and when her plane went higher and higher, he was worried.

"What's she doing?" he cried. "She's gone up to 5,000 feet already! Most new pilots don't go that high for months!"

When Amelia came back down at last, she made a terrible landing. But it did not matter: she was a real pilot now, and after Neta Snook left Kinner Field a while later, Amelia was the only woman there. By December that year, she had her pilot's license, and when she had the money, she was flying as often as she could.

"What do you think?" she asked the other Kinner pilots one afternoon when she arrived at the airfield in a new brown flying coat. They laughed at it because it was new, so for the next few nights she slept in it and put dirt on it.

"Now no one will laugh at me," she thought to herself.

Amelia's sister Muriel was living with her family again now, and she often went to watch Amelia at the airfield. In October 1922, Amelia came home with tickets for an air show for Muriel and her father.

"These tickets are for you," she said. "But I can't sit next to you in the crowd. I'll explain later."

"Perhaps she wants to sit with her friends," Muriel said to her father.

At the show, Edwin and Muriel watched the pilots drive their planes around the airfield. Then suddenly Muriel stood up, her mouth dropping open. "That's the *Canary*!" she cried. "And Amelia is the pilot!"

The *Canary* soon took off and disappeared high into the blue sky. Edwin and Muriel waited for Amelia to come back, feeling more and more worried. "Where's she gone?" they asked each other.

After a very long hour, the *Canary* flew down and landed. Amelia jumped out and ran toward her father and sister at the front of the crowd.

"I just broke the women's altitude record!" she cried to Edwin and Muriel. "I flew to 14,000 feet – higher than any woman has ever flown before!"

A few weeks later, another pilot broke Amelia's altitude record, so she decided to try again. But on the next flight, the weather was not good. Amelia took off from Kinner Field in the *Canary*, and when she got to 10,000 feet, she suddenly saw dark clouds. She was soon flying through heavy snow, and she could not see anything around her.

"What can I do?" she thought, afraid for her life. Then she remembered one of the moves from her aerobatics lessons and quickly put the plane into a fast spin. Down she flew through the snow, faster and faster, toward the ground.

Amelia quickly put the plane into a fast spin.

Chapter 4
An Important Meeting

At 3,000 feet, the plane came out of the heavy snow clouds, and Amelia saw Kinner Field below. She quickly pulled back the control stick and took the *Canary* out of its spin. The plane flew low over the ground, and she landed noisily at the side of the airfield. She did not have her altitude record, but she was alive.

Amelia loved her new life of flying, and she took different jobs to pay for gas, or new parts for her plane. But in the end, it was too expensive, and in the summer of 1923, she sold the *Canary*.

"I'm so sorry to see her go," she said to the young man who bought it. "I've really enjoyed flying her."

"I'm sure I will, too," said the man. "I'm going to take her up right now."

Amelia watched the man walk across to the *Canary* with a friend. They took off into the air, and at once the pilot began to do dangerous aerobatics in the sky.

"What's he doing?" cried one of the other pilots, who was watching with Amelia. The *Canary* flew down fast, too low, and into the ground. It was the end of the *Canary*, and the end of the two young men.

In the spring of 1924, there were problems with Edwin Earhart's business, and problems at home, too. So Amy, Muriel, and Amelia decided to go back east to Boston.

Muriel bought a railroad ticket for herself, but Amelia had other plans. She came home one day in a large, open, yellow car.

"Do you like my new car, Mom? We're going to drive to Boston in it!" she said to her surprised mother.

So Amelia and her mom drove across the United States. They had a wonderful time, and they visited wild and beautiful places like Yellowstone National Park, and even went up into Canada. There were not many cars on the roads in those days, and people ran out of their houses to ask them about their journey and to see the car.

Amelia and her mom drove across the United States.

In Boston, Amelia found interesting work at a place called Denison House. It was a center for people arriving in the United States from other countries, who were often poor and had no work. Here, she taught English, cared for young children, and sometimes took them to the hospital in her car.

She enjoyed her job, but she still wanted to be a pilot, so when she had the money, she flew at an airfield near Boston on weekends. She was always interested in news about flying, too.

One morning, one of the workers at Denison House gave her a newspaper. "Have you seen this, Amelia?" she asked.

SUNDAY MAY 22, 1927

Atlantic record for Lindbergh

Pilot Charles Lindbergh

Brave U.S. pilot Charles Lindbergh has made the first nonstop solo flight across the Atlantic. He flew from New York City to Paris, France in his single-engine plane, the *Spirit of St. Louis*.

The flight was very difficult and dangerous, and at times, Lindbergh needed to fly above terrible storm clouds and through heavy fog. In the past few years, fourteen other people have died trying to make the flight.

In the end, Lindbergh arrived at Le Bourget airport in Paris after thirty-three and a half hours. A crowd of 150,000 excited people were waiting for him there. It was a wonderful welcome for this bright new star of the flying world!

Amelia put down the newspaper. "He's done it! I knew that he would!" she said, smiling. "Now we need a woman to make the same flight!"

About a year later, in April 1928, there was a phone call at Denison House.

"It's for you, Amelia!" said Marion Perkins. She was one of the workers there, and a good friend of Amelia's.

"I can't come to the phone," said Amelia. "I'm busy."

"It's a man called Captain Railey," said Marion. "He says that it's important. He really needs to talk to you now."

Amelia went to the phone. "Good morning, Amelia Earhart speaking," she said.

"Miss Earhart, you don't know me, but my name is Captain Hilton Railey," said the man. "I've heard about your work as a pilot, and I'm calling to ask you a question: Would you like to do something important for the world of flying?"

"What do you mean?" Amelia said.

"Come to my office later," he replied. "Then I can tell you all about it."

That evening, Amelia went with Marion Perkins to Captain Railey's office in Boston.

"Let's get to the important question at once," he said. "Would you like to fly across the Atlantic? No woman has ever done it before – you would be the first!"

Amelia did not reply for a second. "Well... yes, perhaps," she said at last. "But I'll need to know more about it." She did not sound excited – but when Captain Railey looked at her, he saw a light in her eyes.

"Great!" he said. "Then you'll need to meet my friend, George Putnam. He lives in New York."

George Putnam was an important business person who did the publicity for Charles Lindbergh's record flight in 1927. Now, he was looking for a woman who would fly across the Atlantic. He knew that he could make a lot of money from the publicity, but he had to find the right woman.

When Amelia arrived at George Putnam's office in New York, he was in a meeting. She had to wait for a long time before his secretary showed her into his room.

"Miss Earhart," he said. "I've heard so much about you. I'm very pleased to meet you at last."

"And I'm pleased, Mr. Putnam, that your meeting has finished at last," said Amelia drily.

Putnam looked up. He liked at once this bright-faced young woman who was so angry with him.

George Putnam liked at once this bright-faced young woman.

"Let's talk first about the important business," said Putnam, looking at her carefully. "I'm looking for a woman to fly across the Atlantic, and that's why you're here today."

Amelia sat back in her chair with her arms crossed while he explained his plans. His hands were moving all the time, and his face was alive with different ideas. She listened carefully and her face softened a little. He was a very clever man, and she liked that.

By the end of the long meeting, there was a smile on Amelia's face at last. "That sounds very interesting," she said. "You really have thought of everything, Mr. Putnam."

Two days after the meeting in New York, Putnam telephoned Amelia.

"I would like you to be 'Captain' on the cross-Atlantic flight," he told her. "We're going to use a sea plane called the *Friendship* and it will take off from Canada. But you will not fly the plane. There will be two pilots – both men – and we will not pay you anything."

It was not all good news, but it was going to be a great adventure, and Amelia could not possibly say "no".

Chapter 5

Across the Atlantic

For a few weeks, Amelia and the two pilots, Wilmer Stultz and Louis Gordon, were busy getting ready for their Atlantic flight. The flight began in Canada on June 17, and when the great morning came at last, the newspapers were full of stories about what was happening that day. Amelia was surprised to see her name across all the front pages.

When the little orange and gold seaplane took off from the water that exciting morning, Amelia looked up at the sky and smiled to herself.

"Here we go!" she shouted to Stultz and Gordon above the noise of the engine.

The two pilots were sitting at the front of the cockpit, and Gordon turned and smiled at her. "Next stop, Ireland!" he said.

Amelia sat in the back of the plane, next to a little window, writing about the flight in her notebook. She only had the notebook, a watch, a camera, and a warm flying suit. The plane could not be too heavy, so they had only a few things each, and they were not carrying a lot of gas.

At first, the weather was good. But after an hour, the *Friendship* flew into clouds and fog, and then strong winds and a terrible storm. Stultz changed his flying altitude a number of times, and went higher or lower to keep the plane out of danger.

After about eighteen hours, Stultz shouted, "We don't have much gas. We must find the coast of Ireland soon." But the *Friendship* flew on and on, and nobody could see land in the early morning light.

Stultz flew lower over the sea. They were beginning to feel afraid now. There was only an hour's gas, and the radio was not working. They needed to find land soon, or the record, and their lives, were in danger.

Then, at last, Amelia saw something through the little window. "Look, fishing boats!" she shouted. It was a wonderful moment for them all.

Very soon, they saw land. They flew over some small islands and then followed the coast for a while. "I can't see these islands on our maps," said Gordon.

"It doesn't matter. We have to go down now," cried Stultz. "We only have a little gas. We've been in the air for over twenty hours."

Stultz quickly flew down, and they landed on the water near the coast. Nearly twenty-one hours in the air, through fog and storms, and now they had another problem.

"Where is everybody?" laughed Stultz, looking at the empty beach.

After a while, they saw a man, and called to him. The man called back, then disappeared, and after a long time, a different man came out to meet them in a small boat.

They landed on the water near the coast.

"What do you need?" he asked.

"We've just flown across the Atlantic! Are we in Ireland?" they shouted.

"Ireland?" the man laughed. "No, you're near Burry Port in Wales!"

Because of the fog and the storms, the *Friendship* was 100 miles away from Ireland. But it did not matter: Amelia, Stultz, and Gordon were in the United Kingdom, and they had their record.

"Jump into my boat," said the man, "and I'll take you to the coast."

The news about the *Friendship*'s great flight traveled fast, and when Amelia, Stultz, and Gordon walked into Burry Port, there was a crowd of 2,000 excited people waiting for them.

The next day, the three pilots traveled to the town of Southampton on the coast of England, and even bigger crowds were on the streets to welcome them there. Hundreds of reporters pushed around them, and Amelia stood back, surprised and a little afraid at the number of people.

"Miss Earhart, you're the first woman who has ever flown across the Atlantic," cried one of the reporters. "How did you do it?"

"Well, you need to talk to the brave and clever pilots here," replied Amelia. "They flew for over twenty hours in terrible weather. I was just a passenger."

Amelia wanted to talk about Stultz and Gordon and their flying. But the reporters were only interested in Amelia.

"Did you ever think of not coming on the flight?" another reporter asked her.

"Never!" she answered. "I always knew that I wanted to come because I love life and everything that it gives me!"

In Southampton, there were hundreds of messages for Amelia, too – even one from the President of the United States.

The reporters were only interested in Amelia.

From Southampton, Amelia, Stultz, and Gordon went on to London, and after weeks of parties and important dinners, Amelia traveled back to the United States by sea. When she walked off the ship in New York, there was another, even bigger, welcome – and photographers everywhere.

"Miss Earhart!" they cried. "Look over here!"

Amelia was now famous all over the world. George Putnam was very pleased, and he had a lot of publicity plans for her. Amelia's life was suddenly busy.

First, Putnam asked Amelia to write a book about the flight – *20 Hrs. 40 Min. Our Flight in the Friendship*. She also began to work for a weekly women's magazine called *Cosmopolitan*, and many people asked her to give talks about her flying.

With all of this publicity work, Amelia needed to leave her job at Denison House. For the first time in her life, she at last had money, and she could send it home to her mother and sister now, too.

Everybody wanted to hear Amelia's story. In six months, she gave more than one hundred talks in important towns across the country, often flying herself to these places. She even gave a talk at her old high school in Chicago.

At the end, one of the students asked her, "Are you going to write another book next?"

Amelia smiled. "Now, that is an interesting question," she said. "You see, I'm not really a writer. I'm a pilot. And I want to do a lot more flying."

Chapter 6
The Ninety-Nines

Amelia knew some other women pilots by now, and in the spring of 1929, a group of them decided to plan a women's air race. They wanted to do something exciting and different.

"Why don't we have a long race across the country?" said one of the women.

"Great idea," said Amelia. "We can show our work as women pilots to people in different places."

Amelia and her friends planned the race for August 1929. It was called the Women's Air Derby, and the pilots had to fly for eight days across difficult and dangerous country, stopping at a different airfield every day. The end of the race was in Cleveland, Ohio.

But not everybody was excited about the race. Some people thought that flying was too dangerous for women, and one famous person at the race, Will Rogers, laughed at the women pilots.

"Let's call this race 'The Powder Puff Derby!'" he cried.

On August 18, 20,000 people watched the start in Santa Monica, California. They were there to see Amelia and other famous women pilots, like Ruth Nichols and Louise Thaden. But there were problems from the start.

20,000 people watched the start of the Women's Air Derby.

Amelia was flying a new plane, a red Lockheed Vega, which was fast but difficult to fly, and she had an accident at one of the airfields. Luckily, she was unhurt and the plane could still fly, but there was very bad news about another pilot, Marvel Crosson. Her engine stopped over the mountains, and she died when she jumped out. She was one of the many pilots who lost their lives in the world of flying at this time.

Some newspaper reporters wanted the race to end after that. "Can these women really fly planes?" they asked. "Do they know what they are doing?"

But none of the pilots wanted to stop.

"It's even more important for us to go on now," they agreed.

In the end, Louise Thaden was the winner of the Women's Air Derby, and Amelia came in third place. Five women did not finish the long, hard race, but this was not surprising. At that time, the maps were not good, there were no modern altitude or navigation instruments, and planes were often difficult to fly.

"Nineteen women started the race, and fourteen got to the end," said Amelia when she and her friends were talking about it later. "In men's cross-country races, there have never been so many pilots still in the race at the end."

A few days after the race, Amelia met with some of the other women pilots.

"This race has been important for us," she said. "The world now knows that we are good, brave pilots. I was talking with a few of the women this week, and we want to start a special group for women who fly. It would help women pilots in many ways."

Everybody agreed, and on November 2, 1929, the women pilots had their first meeting at an airfield in Long Island, near New York City.

The group was called The Ninety-Nines, because there were ninety-nine women in it at that time, and in 1931, Amelia became its first president. At first, some people laughed at the idea of The Ninety-Nines, but the group soon began to do a lot of important work. It brought women pilots together, helped young women who wanted to learn to fly, and called for equality – for women to have the same things as men.

Amelia was very busy with her flying, but she was also spending more and more time with George Putnam. He helped with many different parts of her publicity, and he even began to tell her what to wear in photographs.

"You and your hats!" he said one day. "You look much better without them."

One day, when people across the United States opened their newspapers, there was an interesting story.

SUNDAY FEBRUARY 8, 1931

Star pilot marries in secret

Amelia Earhart and her husband George Putnam

After months of talk in all of the newspapers, the world's most famous woman pilot, Amelia Earhart, has married George "G.P." Putnam.

They married quietly yesterday at the home of Mr. Putnam's mother in Noank, Connecticut. Miss Earhart wore a skirt suit in her favorite color – brown – but no hat.

George Putnam has done all of Miss Earhart's publicity for the last three years.

We only know three more things about Mr. Putnam and his wife: they will both be back at work tomorrow, Miss Earhart will keep her name, and she will not stop flying. Perhaps she has plans to break more flying records soon.

Chapter 7
Flying Solo

One morning in January 1932, Amelia looked across the breakfast table at her husband.

"I'd like to fly solo across the Atlantic," she said. "No woman has ever done that before. What do you think?"

"I'll always be here to help you, you know that," smiled George, but the coffee cup in his hand shook a little.

They soon began to make plans.

"May 20 is a good day for the flight," George said one evening when they were talking about it. "That date is five years after the Lindbergh flight across the Atlantic. All the newspapers will love that. And since Lindbergh, nobody has done that flight solo."

Amelia already had a cross-Atlantic record, but that one was just as a passenger. This time, she wanted everybody to know that she was a true pilot – and the best woman pilot in the world.

Amelia decided to fly from Newfoundland in Canada, but engineers had to do a lot of work on her Lockheed Vega first. The body of the plane needed to be stronger, to carry a lot of gas, and Amelia also asked them to put in some special modern instruments. One of these could show the plane's altitude.

Before the cross-Atlantic flight, Amelia learned to fly through snow or fog. She did not look out of the window, and used just her instruments.

The weather on the morning of May 20 was not good at first. But mid-morning, George telephoned Amelia from his office. "The weather is good in Newfoundland," he said. "And it looks fine across the Atlantic, too."

So Amelia hurried home, and quickly put on her flying clothes. Before she left, she stopped and looked at all the beautiful flowers in her garden. "Why am I putting my life in danger when I could stay here?" she asked herself, just for a second.

Amelia flew up to Newfoundland with her engineer Bernt Balchen, and then had a short sleep while he and the other engineers got her Lockheed ready. Just after 6:30 that evening, she climbed into the cockpit.

"Do you think that I can do it?" she asked Balchen.

"Sure you can!" he answered, and then he stood back and watched while Amelia started the engine. Minutes later, the Lockheed Vega was climbing into the red evening sky.

At first, everything went well. But then, a few hours into the flight, the altitude instrument stopped working. Now, Amelia did not know how high she was flying. After a while, she went into clouds, so she decided to fly higher to get above them. But soon, she had heavy ice on the wings, and suddenly, the plane went into a fast spin down toward the ocean. Amelia decided to stay in the spin. She knew that when she got lower, the ice would go from the wings. But when she pulled the plane up at last, she could see the gray ocean just below her. Staying in the spin was a clever idea, but it was not without danger.

She flew through the night, sometimes low near the water, sometimes high in the clouds – but each altitude had its problems. When she flew too high, she got ice on her wings and nearly went into a spin again. But when she flew too low, she went into fog. Then, without her altitude instrument, there was a danger that she would hit the water in the dark.

In the early morning, she felt something cold and wet on the back of her neck. It was gas, and it was running into the plane. Amelia now had another worry.

"I don't want a fire on the plane," she thought to herself.

She flew on and on, and at last she saw a boat down below. She knew then that she was near land, and happy and excited, she went in a circle around the boat and then flew on. A few minutes later, she arrived at the coast.

"I've done it!" she cried, looking down at the green land below. She saw a railroad, and decided to follow it.

"It will take me to the nearest town," she thought. "If I'm lucky, there will be an airfield there."

But there was no airfield, and in the end, after flying for nearly fifteen hours, she had to land in a field of cows. Tired but wonderfully happy, she quickly jumped down from the plane. A man was standing watching, his mouth open in surprise.

"Where am I?" she asked.

"In Mr. Gallagher's field," he answered.

"And where's that?" she smiled.

"Near Londonderry, in Northern Ireland," the man said. "Have you come far, Miss?"

"Yes, I have," she laughed. "From the United States!"

"Where am I?" Amelia asked.

Chapter 8
Around the World

Amelia was soon drinking a cup of tea in the man's small house, and Mr. Gallagher, who had a car, then drove her to Londonderry. The police, hearing the news, telephoned the Londonderry newspaper, and soon newspapers around the world knew about Amelia's record. A reporter from one of these newspapers telephoned George.

"Tell her to call me!" he cried excitedly. "I want to hear her voice. She's the greatest woman in the world and I want to tell her that! I've been worried sick all night – tell her to call me at once!"

The next day, Amelia traveled on to London, and when she arrived, the reporters all went wild.

"You're the first woman who has flown solo across the Atlantic," cried one man. "And you're the only person who has flown across it twice! How does it feel?"

"Wonderful," she smiled. "Now people will know that women really can fly and break records."

Another reporter asked, "What are you going to do in London, Miss Earhart?"

"Well, first I'm going to buy some clothes. I couldn't bring any bags, so these are my only clothes!"

Once more, many famous and important people wanted to meet Amelia. The big London store, Selfridges, brought her Lockheed Vega over from Northern Ireland, and thousands of visitors came to see it.

From London, Amelia went to Paris, and George came over to meet her there. They then traveled on together to Italy and Belgium. In every country, important people came to talk to her, and they gave her special presents.

Back in the United States, Amelia had another big welcome from the U.S. President, Herbert Hoover. Her photo was always in the newspapers, but in many ways, she did not change. She was still a friendly person, and happy to talk to the people in the crowds around her.

Amelia finished her second book, which was called *The Fun of It*, just after the cross-Atlantic flight. The name of the book said a lot about Amelia: she always tried to enjoy everything in her life, from flying to giving talks and doing publicity work. That was lucky, because George always had new plans for her.

"The newspapers all think that you wear nice clothes," he said to Amelia one day. "Perhaps we can do business with some of the big stores."

Soon, shoppers at Macy's in New York could buy "clothes by Amelia Earhart". They were for modern women with busy lives, and they were comfortable to wear and easy to wash. Stores across the country sold them for a while, but they did not make very much money. By the end of 1934, Amelia was beginning to think about trying for more flying records.

"I want to fly across the Pacific," she told George one night. "No pilot has ever done that solo."

"Oh... When do you want to do that?" he asked.

"Soon," she said.

Amelia began to make plans at once, and on January 11, 1935, she took off from Hawaii and flew across the Pacific toward California. She had a two-way radio, so many people could listen to her during the flight. They were all excited about her long and dangerous journey, and when she landed in California, thousands of people were waiting for her.

At this time, Amelia was still very busy with talks across the country, and she often spoke about women in the modern world.

"Women can do anything!" she said. "Just like men."

There were many awards for Amelia, too. In the spring of 1935, she won an important award for the best airwoman in the United States.

On top of all this, she began to teach students at Purdue University about flying. Many young women wanted to go to Purdue when they heard that Amelia was working there.

Amelia enjoyed her teaching, but in 1936, she began to think about one last big adventure.

In 1935, Amelia won an important award.

"I'd like to fly around the world," Amelia told George. "I know that other people have done this, but I would be the first woman. It would be one last important record for me."

For her long flight around the world, Amelia needed a special plane, so she bought a big, expensive Lockheed Electra. These planes usually had ten seats, but Amelia took the seats out because she needed to carry more gas. Now, the Electra could fly 3,000 miles nonstop. It also had a modern radio to send messages a long way.

The plane had two engines and it was very difficult to fly, so for about two months Amelia had to have special flying lessons. This long trip was more dangerous than Amelia's other flights, and not all of her friends were happy about it.

"I think that you're possibly going to lose everything with this flight and win nothing," the pilot Louise Thaden said to her.

But Amelia did not listen, and on March 17, 1937, she took off from California with two navigators and flew west to Hawaii on the first part of the trip.

The start of this first round-the-world trip did not go well. When Amelia began to take off from the airfield in Hawaii, the right wing of the Electra suddenly dropped down to one side. She tried to stop the plane, but it moved to the left in a big circle. The wheels broke and fell off, and the body of the plane went along the ground without them. It was a terrible accident for the plane, and terrible for Amelia, too. But it would not stop her.

"Repairing the plane is going to cost us a lot of money," she told George on the telephone later that day. "The Electra won't be ready for another two months. But I still want to make the flight."

Chapter 9
One Last Adventure

Engineers worked hard to repair the plane, and by May 21 it was ready, and Amelia could start her round-the-world flight once more. There were some changes to her plans this second time. She decided to fly east around the world, not west, and she took with her Fred Noonan, a very good navigator and pilot.

George came with her for the first part of the flight, from California to Miami, and he waited with her there for a week while engineers did a few last-minute jobs on the Electra.

While they were in Miami, Amelia talked happily to a reporter. "I think that there is just about one more good flight in me," she smiled. "And I hope that this is it. When I've finished this job, I want to stop these long 'record' flights."

By June 1, 1937, the Electra was ready, and Amelia and Noonan could go on with their flight. Amelia sat on the wing of her plane and said goodbye to George, who looked tired and worried, and then she climbed into the pilot's seat, with Noonan at her side. The engines started noisily, and soon the Electra was racing away across the airfield. George stood and watched while the plane took off, slowly became smaller, and at last disappeared in the early morning sky.

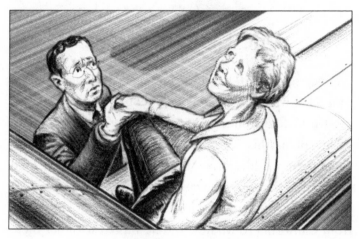

*Amelia sat on the wing of her plane
and said goodbye to George.*

Amelia and Noonan's journey took them down to South America, across the Atlantic to Africa, and then on to India and Thailand.

They landed in Bandung on the island of Java in the middle of June, and George called Amelia soon after they arrived.

"It's so good to hear your voice! How are you?" he asked.

"We're tired. We've flown over 20,000 miles and been in the air for more than 135 hours. But everything is going well, and I think that we're going to be back home by July."

"That's great news!" he said. "We can have a big welcome party for you."

From Bandung, Amelia and Noonan flew down to Australia, arriving in Lae, New Guinea on June 29, ready for the last 7,000 miles of their flight. They were very tired, but now they needed to make the most difficult and dangerous part of their long journey – the nineteen-hour flight to Howland Island.

Amelia talked to Noonan for a long time about their plans. "It's going to be very difficult to find Howland in the ocean – it's only two miles long and half a mile across," she said.

"Don't worry. I know the Pacific well," said Noonan. "And the *Itasca* is waiting for us there. The people on the ship will send us radio messages and help us."

Amelia and Noonan took off from New Guinea

Howland Island

on July 2 at 10:22 a.m., and they said to the people on the *Itasca* that they would arrive at Howland Island early the next morning. For the first seven hours, there were radio messages between the Electra and the radiomen in New Guinea, and Amelia said that everything was fine.

But during the night, there were problems with the

radio messages between the Electra and the *Itasca*. Amelia could only hear one of the messages from the people on the *Itasca*, and they could only hear parts of the messages from her.

"This is a message for Earhart, from the *Itasca*. Where are you?" the *Itasca* radiomen asked again and again, through the night. But there was no reply. When they did get another short message from Amelia, at 7:42 in the morning, she said, "We are not getting messages from you. We think that we are on you, but we cannot see you and we do not have much gas."

The radiomen on the ship tried again and again to speak to Amelia, but she could not hear them. At 8:45, there was one last, short message, and this time Amelia's voice sounded high and worried. "We are flying north and south," she said. Amelia and Noonan were looking for Howland Island, but they could not find it.

Back in the U.S., George was waiting at the Coast Guard station in San Francisco, and by now he was worried sick. While ships began to search the waters around Howland Island, he walked up and down for hours, waiting for news. For the next twenty-four hours, he stayed at the Coast Guard station, listening to reports from the search group – but no one could find the Electra.

George could not rest. The hours became days, and he looked at maps with pilot friends and then telephoned important people at the Coast Guard station.

"Please search the ocean south of Howland Island," he said. "We think that perhaps they have landed there, near the Phoenix Islands."

Sixty-two airplanes flew up and down over the ocean. Boats went out from Howland Island, and the *Itasca* searched for seventeen days, but still there was no news.

June 23, 2013

New photos open Earhart mystery again

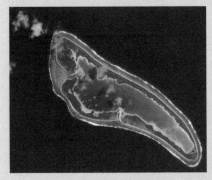

Nikumaroro Island

New underwater photographs have shown something very large which is lying at the bottom of the Pacific Ocean near the island of Nikumaroro. Some people think that it is the plane of world-famous pilot Amelia Earhart. Earhart was trying to become the first woman round-the-world pilot when her Electra plane disappeared over the Pacific in July 1937.

Earhart and her navigator Fred Noonan were flying to Howland Island, in the middle of the Pacific Ocean, when they disappeared. Ships and planes searched the ocean for many days, but nobody ever found the pilots or their plane.

There have been many different stories about what happened in July 1937. Some people said that they saw a man and a woman living on Nikumaroro around this time. They thought that the people looked like the famous pilot and her navigator. But many people think that Earhart and Noonan crashed into the ocean and died when they were looking for Howland Island.

Earhart's husband, George Putnam, went on looking for his wife for years. Perhaps now we will find out what really happened to this extraordinary woman. She was one of the greatest pilots of her time, and an example to women everywhere.

GLOSSARY

aerobatics *(n)* exciting moves that a plane makes

air *(n)* the space around and above things

altitude *(n)* how high something is above the sea; a place that is high above the sea

award *(n)* money etc. that you give to somebody who has done something very well

become *(v)* to begin to be something (past tense **became**)

boot *(n)* a shoe that covers your foot and ankle and sometimes part of your leg

brave *(adj)* not afraid to do dangerous or difficult things

coast *(n)* the land that is next to the sea

Coast Guard *(n)* a person who watches the sea and ships and helps people who are in danger

cockpit *(n)* the part of a plane that a pilot sits in

controls *(n)* parts of a machine; when you push or move the controls, the machine works

derby *(n)* an important race (named after an English horse race)

disappear *(v)* If a person or thing disappears, they go away so people cannot see them.

engine *(n)* a machine; it makes things move

extraordinary *(adj)* very unusual or strange

fair *(adj)* light in colour

flight *(n)* a trip in an airplane

fog *(n)* cloud near the ground; it is difficult to see through

gas *(n)* A car or plane needs this to drive or fly.

goggles *(n)* big glasses that stop things getting in your eyes

helmet *(n)* a hard hat that keeps your head safe

ice *(n)* water that has become hard because it is colder than 0 degrees C

idea *(n)* a new plan

instrument *(n)* something that you use in a car, plane, or ship to see how far, fast, high, etc. you are going

land *(v)* to come down from the air to the ground; *(n)* the part of the Earth that is not the ocean

license *(n)* a piece of paper that shows you can do something

low *(adj)* near the ground

map *(n)* a picture of a place that shows things like mountains, rivers, and roads; you use it to find your way somewhere

message *(n)* words that one person sends to another

navigator *(n)* a person who decides which way a plane, ship, or car should go

nonstop *(adj)* without a stop or a rest

ocean *(n)* the salt water over most of the Earth

pilot *(n)* a person who flies an airplane

playsuit *(n)* clothes that children wear to play in

powder puff *(n)* something that you use for putting powder on your face, to make yourself more beautiful

president *(n)* the most important person in a group of people and in many countries

problem *(n)* something that is difficult; something that you worry about

publicity *(n)* information that tells everyone about a person or thing; the job of giving this information

race *(n)* In a race you try to run, drive, etc. faster than other people.

railroad *(n)* trains; the metal lines that they go on; and the businesses that own them

record *(n)* the best, fastest, highest, lowest, etc. in a sport

repair *(v)* to make something that is broken good again

reporter *(n)* a person who writes in a newspaper or speaks on the radio or television about things that have happened

search *(v)* to look carefully because you are trying to find someone or something

shed *(n)* a small building; you keep things in it

sled *(n)* a small box on pieces of metal or wood, which you sit in to move over snow

solo *(adj)* alone; without other people

take off When an airplane takes off, it leaves the ground and begins to fly (past tense **took off**)

toward *(prep)* on the way to something

uncle *(n)* the brother of your mother or father, or the husband of your aunt

university *(n)* People go to university to learn after they have left high school or college.

war *(n)* fighting between countries or between groups of people

welcome *(adj)* If someone or something is welcome, you are happy to see them or it.

win *(v)* to be the best or the first in a game or race (past tense **won**)

THE HISTORY OF FLIGHT

◀ 1783

Jean-Francois Pilâtre de Rozier and the Francois Laurent d'Arlandes make the first flight in a hot-air balloon in Paris.

1903 ▶

The Wright brothers make the first flight in a plane at Kitty Hawk, North Carolina, in the United States.

◀ 1909

Louis Blériot flies across the English Channel.

1911 ▶

Calbraith P. Rodgers flies across the United States.

◀ **1919**

John Alcock and Arthur Whitten Brown make the first nonstop flight across the Atlantic.

1927 ▶

Charles Lindbergh makes the first solo nonstop flight across the Atlantic.

◀ **1933**

Wiley Post makes the first solo flight around the world. It takes three days, twenty-two hours, and one minute.

1939 ▶

Pan American World Airways make the first cross-Atlantic passenger flight from New York City to Southampton.

ACTIVITIES

Before Reading

1 **Match the words below to their meanings.**

disappear   flight   message   navigator   pilot

1 a person who flies a plane
2 a trip in a plane
3 words that one person sends to another
4 when someone goes away and no one can see them
5 a person who decides which way a plane, ship, or car should go

2 **Look at the title, front cover, and back cover. Answer the questions.**

1 Who was Amelia Earhart?
2 What kind of person do you think she was?
3 Why did she become famous?
4 What did she want to do after her last flight?

3 **What do you think happens on Amelia's last important flight? Choose the best answer.**

1 She breaks a new record.
2 She decides never to fly again.
3 She flies into bad weather and cannot finish the flight.
4 She and her plane disappear.

ACTIVITIES

While Reading

Foreword

Circle the correct words in each sentence.

1 Amelia Earhart's plane has disappeared in the *Pacific / Atlantic* Ocean.
2 She was flying *across Europe / around the world.*
3 She was flying with a *navigator / her husband.*
4 A ship called the *Itasca* was waiting for Earhart's plane *in New Guinea / at Howland Island.*

Chapter 1

Are these sentences true or false?

1 Amelia and her sister make a ride with their uncle.
2 Amelia does not want to go on the ride.
3 Edwin Earhart spends a lot of time with his daughters.
4 After 1914, Amelia's family move home many times.

Chapter 2

1 Put the events in order.

1 Amelia goes up in a plane for the first time.
2 Amelia leaves her college in Philadelphia.
3 Amelia talks to her father about flying lessons.
4 A plane flies at Amelia during an air show.

2 Choose the correct words.

1 Amelia *works / studies* at a hospital in Canada.
2 Amelia lives with her *parents / sister* in California.
3 Amelia's father buys her a *plane ride / flying lesson*.
4 Frank Hawks thinks Amelia *will / will not* be afraid.

Chapter 3

1 Answer these questions about the people in the story.

1 Who gives Amelia her first flying lesson?
2 Who gives Amelia money to buy her first plane?
3 Who gives Amelia exciting aerobatics lessons?
4 Who goes to the air show with Amelia's father?

2 Complete the sentences with *loves*, *likes*, or *does not like*.

1 When Neta Snook meets Amelia, she _____ her.
2 Edwin Earhart _____ the idea of flying lessons.
3 Amy Earhart _____ short hair on women.
4 Amelia _____ flying in her plane, the *Canary*.

Chapter 4

1 Are these sentences true or false?

1 Amelia drives to Boston alone in a yellow car.
2 Lindbergh was the first person to fly alone across the Atlantic without stopping in May 1927.
3 George Putnam did the publicity for Lindbergh's flight.
4 He asks Amelia to be the pilot of the *Friendship*.

2 What happens when Amelia meets George Putnam? Choose one answer.

a She likes him at once, and is interested in his ideas.

b She is angry with him, and leaves the meeting early.

c She is angry with him at first, but soon sees that he has interesting and clever ideas.

Chapter 5

1 Complete these sentences with the correct names.

1 _____ sits in the back of the *Friendship*.

2 _____ lands the *Friendship* not far from the coast.

3 _____ sends Amelia a message in Southampton.

4 _____ asks Amelia to write a book.

2 What does Amelia do? Write *Yes* or *No*.

1 She flies back to the United States from London.

2 She begins to work for a weekly magazine.

3 She goes back to her usual job after the record flight.

4 She travels to different towns and talks about flying.

Chapter 6

Put the events in order.

1 Amelia and other women pilots start The Ninety-Nines.

2 Amelia marries George Putnam in Connecticut.

3 Marvel Crosson has a terrible accident.

4 The Women's Air Derby begins in California.

Chapter 7

Are these sentences true or false?

1 Amelia begins her flight on the same date as Lindbergh.
2 There are problems with ice on the plane's wings.
3 Amelia flies from Newfoundland to the south of England.
4 Amelia flies nonstop for nearly fifteen hours.

Chapter 8

What does Amelia do? Write *Yes* or *No*.

1 She meets George in London.
2 She writes her third book when she returns to the U.S.
3 She teaches university students about flying.
4 She makes the first solo flight across the Pacific.
5 She begins to plan a trip around the world.

Chapter 9

Put the events in order.

1 George and Amelia talk on the phone.
2 George and Amelia say goodbye in Miami.
3 Amelia and Noonan fly to Bandung.
4 Photos show something large in the Pacific Ocean.
5 The *Itasca* gets a last message from Amelia.

ACTIVITIES

After Reading

Vocabulary

1 Replace the underlined words with the words below.

extraordinary   low   non stop   solo   take off   win

1 He plans to fly <u>alone</u>.
2 She is going to <u>be first in</u> the race.
3 The pilot was flying very <u>near the ground</u>.
4 They flew <u>without stopping</u> for fifteen hours.
5 My plane will <u>leave the airfield</u> at 8:30.
6 Amelia Earhart was an <u>unusual</u> person.

2 Complete the sentences with the correct words.

award   fog   idea   map   race   reporter   war

1 I couldn't find the station so I looked at my _____.
2 He ran very fast and he came first in the _____.
3 We couldn't see the road because of the _____.
4 Our grandfather fought in the _____ a long time ago.
5 My uncle works for a newspaper. He's a _____.
6 At first, I didn't know what to do, but then I suddenly had a good _____.
7 She worked very hard at school last year and she won a special _____.

Grammar

1 **Complete the sentences using the infinitive (e.g. *to work*) or the *-ing* form (e.g. *working*). Use the words in brackets.**

Amelia needed _____ (take) the plane out of the spin.
Amelia needed to take the plane out of the spin.

1 Amy decided _____ (make) playsuits for her daughters.
2 Muriel always enjoyed _____ (play) with her sister.
3 Amelia learned _____ (fly) the new plane very quickly.
4 Amelia finished _____ (study) at Philadelphia in 1917.
5 Amelia asked George _____ (help) her with the flight.
6 A lot of girls wanted _____ (go) to Purdue University.
7 George remembered _____ (meet) the reporter before.

2 **Write sentences with the comparative of the word in brackets.**

The Lockheed Vega was faster than the *Canary*.
The Canary was slower than the Lockheed Vega. (slow)

1 George Putnam was older than Amelia.
Amelia _____. (young)
2 Driving lessons are cheaper than flying lessons.
Flying lessons _____. (expensive)
3 The *Canary* was quieter than the Electra.
The Electra _____. (noisy)
4 The weather in Canada is worse than the weather here.
The weather here _____. (good)

Reading

1 Read each sentence and write:
a) who says it to Amelia.
b) what they are talking about.

1 "Amelia, you nearly died!"
2 "I just don't have the money."
3 "I think you're going to be good at this."
4 "I'm calling to ask you a question."
5 "There will be two pilots – both men – and we will not pay you anything."
6 "I think that you're possibly going to lose everything with this flight and win nothing."
7 "Don't worry. I know the Pacific well."

2 Look at Chapters 8 and 9 and complete the sentences with the correct numbers.

1 Amelia won an award for flying in the spring of _____.
2 Lockheed Electra planes usually had _____ seats.
3 The Electra had _____ engines so it was hard to fly.
4 Amelia and Noonan flew _____ miles around the world from the United States to Bandung.
5 George wanted to have a party on July _____.
6 It was a _____-hour flight from New Guinea to Howland Island.
7 _____ planes helped to search for the Electra.
8 The *Itasca* looked for Amelia's plane for _____ days.

Writing

1 Read the article. Find and correct three mistakes in it.

> ### JUNE 18 1928
>
> # *First woman flies across Atlantic*
>
> Amelia Earhart has crossed the Atlantic in the plane the *Friendship* with American pilots Wilmer Stultz and Frank Hawks. She is the first woman who has ever flown across the Atlantic.
>
> The flight was very long and dangerous. The orange and gold plane left from Canada and was in the air for nearly twenty-six hours. The radio stopped working and the pilots needed to fly through fog and terrible storms. But in the end they arrived safely near the small town of Burry Port in Ireland.

2 Plan an article about Amelia's solo flight across the Atlantic. First, look at Chapter 7 and make notes about:

the new flying record
how long the flight was
the name / color / type of plane
the weather / any problems during the flight
where the plane left from / landed

3 Use your notes to write an article about the flight. Think of an interesting headline to go at the top.

Speaking

1 **Read the phrases. Underline the language used to compare.**

1 Flying was a lot more dangerous when Amelia Earhart was a pilot...

2 Getting publicity was much easier in the 1920s...

3 Flying was more interesting in the early days...

4 Sending messages was much more difficult in the 1930s...

2 **Now match the phrases in exercise 1 to the phrases below. Do you agree with the sentences? Why / Why not? Talk to a partner about them.**

a ... because the planes often had problems.

b ... because the radios often didn't work very well.

c ... because planes were new and exciting.

d ... because there weren't many famous people.

3 **Complete these sentences with your own words. Say them to a partner. Do they agree? Why / Why not?**

1 Driving was... in the early days because...

2 Traveling abroad was... in the 1920s because...

3 Finding out new things was... thirty years ago because...

4 Being a woman was... in the 1930s because...

5 Living now is... because...

THE OXFORD BOOKWORMS LIBRARY

THE OXFORD BOOKWORMS LIBRARY is a best-selling series of graded readers which provides authentic and enjoyable reading in English. It includes a wide range of original and adapted texts: classic and modern fiction, non-fiction, and plays. There are more than 250 Bookworms to choose from, in seven carefully graded language stages that go from beginner to advanced level.

Each Bookworm is illustrated, and offers extensive support, including:

▸ a glossary of above-level words
▸ activities to develop language and communication skills
▸ notes about the author and story
▸ online tests

Each Bookworm pack contains a reader and audio.

6	**STAGE 6**	▸ 2500 HEADWORDS	▸ CEFR B2–C1
5	**STAGE 5**	▸ 1800 HEADWORDS	▸ CEFR B2
4	**STAGE 4**	▸ 1400 HEADWORDS	▸ CEFR B1–B2
3	**STAGE 3**	▸ 1000 HEADWORDS	▸ CEFR B1
2	**STAGE 2**	▸ 700 HEADWORDS	▸ CEFR A2–B1
1	**STAGE 1**	▸ 400 HEADWORDS	▸ CEFR A1–A2
S	**STARTER**	▸ 250 HEADWORDS	▸ CEFR A1

Find a full list of *Bookworms* and resources at
www.oup.com/elt/gradedreaders

If you liked this stage 2 Bookworm, why not try...

Grace Darling
TIM VICARY

The *Forfarshire* was wrecked off the north-east coast of England on a stormy night in 1838. This is the story of Grace Darling – a girl who became a famous heroine.